10-minute
SEASONAL
CRAFTS
for
SUMMER

ANNALEES LIM

WINDMILL
BOOKS

New York

Published in 2015 by Windmill Books, An Imprint of Rosen Publishing
29 East 21st Street, New York, NY 10010

Senior Editor for Wayland: Julia Adams
US Editor: Joshua Shadowens
Craft stylist: Annalees Lim
Designer: Emma Randall
Photographer: Simon Pask, N1 Studios

Photo Credits: All step-by-step craft photography: Simon Pask, N1 Studios; images used throughout for creative graphics: Shutterstock.

Library of Congress Cataloging-in-Publication Data

Lim, Annalees, author.
 10-minute seasonal crafts for summer / by Annalees Lim.
     pages cm. — (10-minute seasonal crafts)
 Includes index.
 ISBN 978-1-4777-9210-0 (library binding) — ISBN 978-1-4777-9211-7 (pbk.) —
ISBN 978-1-4777-9212-4 (6-pack)
1. Handicraft—Juvenile literature. 2. Summer—Juvenile literature. I. Title. II. Title: Summer.
TT160.L48494 2015
745.5—dc23

                              2013048368

Manufactured in the United States of America

CPSIA Compliance Information: Batch # WS14WM: For Further Information contact Windmill Books, New York, New York at 1-866-478-0556

Contents

Summer

The year is made up of four seasons – winter, spring, summer and autumn. Each season lasts for about three months. Summer lasts from June to August.

Summer is the time of year when everything is in full bloom and the Sun is at its hottest. It's time for holidays and having lots of fun outside! Trips to the beach, picnics in the park and playing outside with friends are some of the things that make summer so much fun.

There are so many exciting things to find in nature during the summer, and this book can tell you what to make with them – in only 10 minutes! Just remember to be careful about what you collect. Plants and flowers are living things and should not be picked without permission. Anything that you do collect should be washed before you use it.

All the projects in this book are inspired by the fun you can have when you are in the great outdoors. If you are playing outside, or visiting the seaside or countryside, always remember to wear sunscreen.

Crawling Crabs

Beaches are sometimes very busy and it's hard to see anything other than people. Don't forget that there are many creatures that live in and around the sea. Crawling crabs like to hide among the rocks. Why not make your own using shells that you find at the beach?

You will need:

- A round, flat shell
- Red acrylic paint
- 4 red pipe cleaners
- Tape
- Googly eyes
- Glue

1 Use soapy water and a sponge to clean your shell.

2 Take four red pipe cleaners and twist them together in the middle.

3

Stick the pipe cleaners to the inside of the shell using tape.

4

Paint the shell with red acrylic paint.

5

Bend the six legs and the two pincers into shape. Glue some googly eyes onto the shell.

Butterfly Clothespins

Summer means that all the caterpillars from spring will emerge from their cocoons as beautiful butterflies! Butterflies don't make great pets, but they are fantastic to look at. Make some of your own that you can keep and hang up just by using some leaves and pipe cleaners.

1 Choose four leaves that you like, making sure that two are large and two are small.

2 Cover both sides of these leaves with a layer of tape, then cut around the leaves.

3

Stick the leaves onto the clothespin with glue. These will make the butterfly wings.

4

Use a pipe cleaner to make a body and curly antennae. Stick this onto the clothespin.

5

Decorate the leaf wings with some foam shapes or stickers.

Seascape in a Bottle

Take a peek at what lurks under the sea without even getting wet! Collect some sand, shells and stones from your trip to the beach to make a fantastic keepsake of the day.

You will need:

- Small plastic bottle with lid
- Sand, shells and stones
- Water (you could even collect some seawater)
- Blue food coloring
- Green and orange paper
- Broad tape
- Scissors

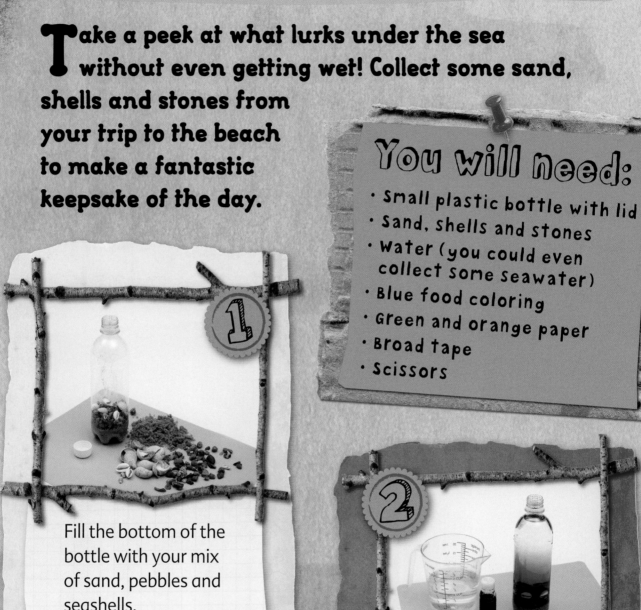

1 Fill the bottom of the bottle with your mix of sand, pebbles and seashells.

Fill your bottle with other fun things. You could make a small modeling clay diver or even sprinkle in some glitter, so that it looks like the Sun's rays catching the ripples on the sea.

2 Fill the bottle with water and add a few drops of blue food coloring. Then screw the lid on tightly.

Cut out shapes of fish and seagrass to decorate your bottle.

Create an underwater scene by securing your cut out shapes to the back of the bottle with tape.

3

4

11

Sandcastles

Sandcastles are great to make on a sandy beach, but there is no way you could ever take them home with you! With this craft, you can take home some of the sand you used and recreate your favorite beach builds.

You will need:
- card stock
- colored paper
- Scissors
- Pen
- Sand
- Glue
- Small bowl
- Paintbrush

1 Decorate a piece of card stock with sand and sea cut from paper.

2 Draw a sandcastle shape onto the card stock.

Why not try making other sand creations, too, such as people, animals and buildings.

3

In a bowl, mix equal quantities of sand and glue.

4

Using a paintbrush, fill the whole sandcastle shape with a thin layer of the sandy glue.

5

Decorate the top of the sandcastle with a bright flag made from paper.

Flower Prints

Many flowers are in bloom in the summer, but once you pick them they don't last for very long. Choose some flowers that you like to make a pretty flower picture you can hang on your wall.

You will need:

- Flowers
- Any water-based paint
- Piece of cardboard
- Paintbrush
- Colored paper
- Scissors
- Glue stick

1

Pick some summery flowers. Make sure you check with an adult before picking them.

2

Paint a thin layer of paint onto a flat surface, such as a piece of cardboard.

3

Gently press the flower into the paint and then print it onto a brightly colored piece of paper.

4

Use different colors and types of flowers to make a large flower picture.

5

When your picture is dry, you can cut the flower out and glue onto another bright piece of paper, so you can hang it on the wall.

You could decorate some sticks with paper leaves and use them as stems for your flowers!

Mini Kites

Do you like flying kites in the summer? When it's not windy enough to let yours soar, you could try making these mini kites to decorate your bedroom.

1 Find four twigs, two longer and two shorter.

2 Working on a piece of plastic, cover part of the tissue paper with a thin layer of glue. Lay the sticks onto the glued area in the shape of a kite.

Make lots of these kites and tie them onto some string so that you can hang them at the window. The tissue paper will act like stained glass and make lovely colored light when the Sun shines through it.

3

Add two more sticks to make the cross in the kite.

4

Place a piece of string at the bottom of the kite and tie some bows onto it with more string.

5

Using more glue, fold the excess tissue paper over to cover the sticks. Decorate your kite with tissue paper shapes. Leave to dry.

Sunflower Pot

Lots of people grow sunflowers in the summer and compete with others to see how high they can grow them! If you can't grow your own, have a go at making a sunflower using real sunflower seeds.

You will need:

- Sunflower seeds
- Yellow and orange felt
- Pen
- Scissors
- Paper
- Glue
- Old pot or jelly jar with lid

1 Draw one small and one large petal shape onto a piece of paper. Cut them out to make two templates.

2 Use the large template to draw six petals onto a piece of yellow felt. Use the small template to draw six petals onto the orange felt.

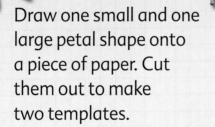

Try making a poppy, too! Use red felt for the petals and real poppy seeds for the center.

3

Cut out all 12 petals using the scissors.

4

Stick the petals onto the lid using glue.

5

Glue the sunflower seeds into the center of the lid. Leave to dry, and then decorate your pot with strips of colored card stock.

Rafts

Have you ever raced a boat down a river before? It's great fun, especially if you do it with your friends. You could each make a raft like this one and see which one can race the fastest!

You will need:

- Sticks
- String
- A leaf
- Tape
- Scissors

1
Collect six sticks that are the same length.

2
Tie all the sticks together by using string. Start by taking a long piece of string, folding it in half and tying it to one stick.

3

Tie a knot around each stick with string as you tie them together. Repeat this on the other side.

4

Create a mast by tying four pieces of string to the end of a stick. Tie the end of each string to a corner of the raft.

5

Find a small leaf to make a flag. Before you stick it on, cover it with tape. Now you can race your raft!

Starfish

You don't always have to make craft projects indoors. You can make this seaside keepsake when you are on a sandy beach or when you are playing in a sandbox.

You will need:

- Sandy beach or sandbox
- Powdered plaster
- Water (or seawater)
- Shells and pebbles
- String
- Jug
- Mixing stick

1

Press a starfish shape into the sand using your fingers or a cookie cutter.

2

Decorate the inside of the starfish by using some small shells and pebbles.

You can make this craft at the beach. Just take the powdered plaster with you in a ziplock bag and pour the seawater in when you are ready. Close the bag and shake well to mix the plaster.

3 Mix some plaster in a jug using powdered plaster and water. Check the plaster packet for exact measurements.

4 Pour the plaster mix into the starfish shape.

5 Place a loop of string into the plaster at the top of the starfish and leave to dry for an hour.

Glossary

excess (EK-ses) Something that is left over.

keepsake (KEEP-sayk) An item that is kept as a memory of a place or person.

recreate (ree-kree-AYT) To make or build a copy of something.

ripples (RIH-pulz) Small waves.

template (TEM-plut) Shape you can draw around again and again to make the same shape.

tissue paper (TIH-shoo PAY-per) Very thin paper, often used as wrapping paper.

Index

Further Reading

Barnham, Kay. *Summer*. Seasons. New York: PowerKids Press, 2011.

Lim, Annalees. *Fun with Nature*. Clever Crafts. New York, Windmill Books, 2013.

Websites

For web resources related to the subject of this book, go to: www.windmillbooks.com/weblinks and select this book's title.